Cindy Morgan:

Beyond the Grid - Exploring the Life and Legacy of a Tron Icon

Shawn C.Lister

Cindy Morgan

Cindy Morgan

TABLE OF CONTENTS

Cindy Morgan

Cindy Morgan

INTRODUCTION

Cindy Morgan became a bright star in the glittering world of neon and pixels, where algorithms dance in the circuitry and code seeps into reality. She gave Lora and Yori life, bringing them to life beyond the digital landscapes and grid of special effects, leaving a lasting impression on the history of science fiction film. Morgan's career has stretched from radio waves to silver screens, and he has inspired many others with his brilliance, persistence, and unbreakable spirit. His journey goes beyond Tron's ground-breaking graphics.

This book is more than just a biography; it's a key to unlocking Cindy Morgan's complex universe and a decoder ring. We explore the early years that influenced her artistic development, following her journey from radio prodigy to Hollywood's golden girl. We traverse the thrilling landscape of Tron's creation, removing the

Cindy Morgan

layers of technical magic to uncover the passion and
emotion Morgan invested in her two parts.

However, our adventure doesn't finish within the grid.
We go further, delving into the varied terrain of Morgan's
television career, her humorous roles in movies such as
Caddyshack, and her lasting influence in the
ever-changing entertainment industry. We get to know
the lady behind the screen and learn about her steadfast
devotion to charity and women's empowerment.

Cindy Morgan: Beyond the Grid is proof of the
transformational potential of an actress who didn't
hesitate to challenge conventions and push the envelope.
It honors her adaptability, tenacity, and the lasting
influence she has left in the annals of popular culture.
Come along with us as we unravel the secrets around the
icon and uncover the personal brightness that shines
through the pixels as we sail the thrilling river of her life.
Immerse yourself in Cindy Morgan's narrative and be
ready to be astounded.

CHAPTER 1: CHILDHOOD

Cindy Morgan: Hollywood Lights to Chicago Streets

The beginning of Cindy Morgan's narrative takes place on the harsh streets of Chicago rather than in a glistening digital setting. She was reared in a working-class Polish-German household, far from the glitz and glitter of Hollywood, after being born Cynthia Ann Cichorski in 1954. However, she had a glimmer of inventiveness that was stoked by vivid dreams and bedtime tales.

She gained a strong work ethic and compassion that she carried with her throughout her life from her experience attending Catholic institutions. Her playground at Northern Illinois University was the radio. As a DJ, she

Cindy Morgan

developed her ability to engage crowds by spinning
songs and enticing them with her contagious enthusiasm.

However, Morgan found himself drawn to television and
movies due to their alluring images and powerful stories.
Driven by a desire to share tales that went beyond radio
broadcasts, she took on the stage name "Cindy Morgan,"
a reference to the legendary sorceress Morgan le Fay,
and bravely embarked on her Hollywood career.

Despite seeming to be a world apart from Tron's digital
grid, Morgan's early existence had a significant impact
on his path. Her love of storytelling and her ability to
engage audiences served as her compass, while the
principles of her upbringing served as her fulcrum. We'll
look at how these same traits launched her career and
helped her get famous parts that cemented her place in
pop culture history in the next chapter.

1.1. Professional Experience

Cindy Morgan: Getting Around Hollywood's Maze

Cindy Morgan's career developed as if it were a multi-layered map, with each turn guiding her through various entertainment business domains. She worked hard in her early years, moving from radio DJ to weather lady to commercial star. She became well-known throughout the country thanks to the Irish Spring Girl campaign, but Morgan wanted more than flimsy commercials.

Her breakthrough performance was in the 1980 comedy classic "Caddyshack." Morgan, who starred as the exuberant Lacey Underall, brought a charming and naive character to life. Her sparkling personality and hilarious timing stole the show. As a result of her popularity, she was able to pursue television parts, including lead roles in the enduring serial opera "Falcon Crest" and cameos in programs like "Matlock" and "Amazing Stories."

But science fiction was the realm that solidified Morgan's historical legacy. She made her feature film debut in 1982 in "Tron." She demonstrated her depth and adaptability in her twin roles as Yori, her digital avatar, and Lora, the human coder. She not only skillfully handled the film's technical difficulties, but she also gave these opposing characters a compelling sense of compassion and subtlety.

Morgan kept performing over the years, but her career did not follow the conventional Hollywood route. In addition to exploring production and collaborating on other movies, she also embraced her altruistic side and directed charity events such as the Caddyshack Reunion Golf Tournament. Her many interests and unshakable determination to utilize her position for good were mirrored in this diversified approach.

A tapestry of comedy, drama, and a hint of future magic characterized Cindy Morgan's career. She forged a route that cut across genres and connected with viewers of all ages by navigating the turbulent Hollywood landscape with poise and fortitude. We'll go into more detail about her legacy and her long-lasting influence on the entertainment industry in the next chapter.

1.2. Instruction

Cindy Morgan: Chicago Was the Spark, Education Was the Fire

The beginning of Cindy Morgan's tale takes place on the busy streets of Chicago rather than in the glistening Tron pixels. She was reared in a working-class Polish-German household, far from the glitter and glamor of Hollywood, after being born Cynthia Ann Cichorski in 1954. Nonetheless, a creative spark that was sparked by her early life and scholastic experiences began to ignite inside her.

Constructing the Brick by Brick of Imagination:

Her education in Catholic schools established a solid basis, imbuing her with a sense of self-control and compassion. These principles would serve her well throughout her life, directing her dealings with both coworkers and admirers. But her vivid imagination could not be contained inside the classroom walls. Morgan was a voracious reader who would lose herself in the exploits of made-up characters. Her passion for storytelling from an early age served as the inspiration for her professional path.

Discovering Her Voice

Cindy Morgan

When Morgan arrived at Northern Illinois University, her passion for communication had grown. She assumed the character of a DJ and turned the airwaves into her playground. Morgan developed her ability to engage audiences in this setting, where her contagious energy and easy interaction with the listeners won her over. She learned how to engage a varied audience and effectively transmit emotion from this experience, which turned out to be priceless.

A Star Is Born—And Given a Name:

Radio provided a venue, but Morgan had greater ideas for stories—stories that would include more than simply voices—such as images and feelings. Driven by this aspiration, she made a risky decision and acquired the stage name "Cindy Morgan," after the legendary sorceress Morgan le Fay. Her transition from a simple radio personality to an aspiring actor prepared to take on the worlds of cinema and television was marked by this rebranding.

Cindy Morgan

Despite seeming to be a world apart from Tron's digital grid, Morgan's Chicago background had a significant impact on who she is. Her enthusiasm for storytelling and her ability to connect with audiences drove her onward, while the principles she learned in school served as her compass. We'll look at how these same traits launched her career and helped her get famous parts that cemented her place in pop culture history in the next chapter.

.

CHAPTER 2: RADIO BEGINNING

Cindy Morgan: Creating Waves From Radio to Cinema

The tale of Cindy Morgan didn't start in Tron's flashing neon grid; instead, it sparked and crackled on Chicago's radio waves. Born in 1954 as Cynthia Ann Cichorski, her dreams extended beyond the busy streets outside her window. But before the lights of Hollywood, there were records playing and radio microphones.

Classroom to Console:

Cindy Morgan

Discipline and a strong work ethic were instilled in her throughout her Catholic school education; these traits would later help her navigate the rigorous Hollywood industry. Beneath the teachings and prayers, Morgan's mind was busy creating. She experienced storytelling firsthand as a youngster, and it was more than simply a literary device.

Morgan's first outlet for this enthusiasm came when she enrolled at Northern Illinois University to pursue a degree in communications. But her inventiveness was too much for the blank pages of textbooks. The radio called to her, its undefinable waves offering a platform for her developing narrative skills.

Telling Stories and Holding Audiences' Attention:

She became a DJ with a glint in her eye and a hint of young bravado. Morgan became a master storyteller behind the microphone, weaving tales out of music and stories that enthralled audiences. Through the airways, her voice—infused with contagious energy and inherent charisma—painted vivid visions.

This was about engaging with people, sharing experiences, and opening their eyes to a world of possibilities—it was much more than simply spinning CDs and playing popular tunes. Morgan developed her improvisational and audience-engaging talents, which she would later apply to the film with ease.

Past the Dial:

But the radio waves were too limiting for her aspirations. Film and television, with their rich emotional content and intricate visual designs, beckoned to her like sirens. Equipped with the self-assurance bestowed by her radio triumph and the innate storytelling abilities she had been raised with, Cindy Morgan was prepared to take the stage.

She did, however, take on a new identity before the bright lights of Hollywood: Cindy Morgan. This stage name was inspired by the fabled sorceress Morgan le Fay. This was more than just conceit; it was a symbolic removal of her radio persona and a proclamation of her determination to rule the realm of cinematic narrative.

We'll look at how Morgan's radio-honed ability and the flame that was lit in Chicago led to her legendary parts and solidified her position in pop culture history in the next chapter. Tune in for an experience that will take you from radio to big screens, from seductive whispers to jaw-dropping performances.

2.1. Acting Transition

Cindy Morgan: From FM Broadcasting to Hollywood Stardom

Cindy Morgan

Cindy Morgan's path did not happen overnight, moving from urban streets to neon-lit screens. Her unwavering desire for storytelling and her radio-forged skill drove her step by step along the steady ascent. Behind the scenes, the charismatic DJ underwent a makeover and became a self-assured actor.

Giving Up the Mic and Taking Up the Camera:

Morgan stepped out of the radio booth and headed for the bright lights of Los Angeles, leaving behind the comforting familiarity of Chicago. Her playground, the radio, seemed limiting. TV and movies beckoned like a siren's call, with their capacity to weave visual tales and paint emotions.

Perfecting Your Craft:

Morgan decided to take acting courses, armed with the unyielding dedication she had developed throughout her radio days. She devoured screenplays, became well-versed in industry practices, and developed a strong

Cindy Morgan

sense of character inhabiting. Her radio days provided her with contagious enthusiasm and improvisational talents that were crucial in molding her ability to engage audiences and bring life to a variety of roles.

Weather Girl to Irish Spring Queen in Transition

There were difficulties with the move. Starting from nothing, Morgan obtained her first jobs anywhere she could, such as a local station's weather girl and an auto show representative for Fiat. Every chance she had, no matter how little, helped her grow as a professional and hone her on-camera presence.

The Irish Spring Girl campaign was the turning point that followed. Morgan's charisma and inherent attractiveness had her appear in ads that were shown in homes all around the country. The catalyst for her to seek bigger jobs in Hollywood was her national notoriety, which served as the key to unlocking the doors.

Having Confidence While Facing the Camera:

Cindy Morgan

It was in 1980 that the world first saw "Lacey Underall," the effervescent beauty from the comedy classic "Caddyshack." Morgan's outstanding screen presence and hilarious timing made her the star of the program. This was more than simply a part; it was an announcement of her coming and a recognition of her skill and hard work.

Cindy Morgan's path from radio waves to Hollywood screens wasn't a storybook; rather, it was an ode to her undying enthusiasm, her never-ending pursuit of knowledge, and her self-assurance in pursuing her ambition. We'll examine her legacy and the legendary roles that solidified her position in pop culture history in the next chapter.

2.2. The important role

Ah, the moment of discovery! That critical moment in pop culture history when an artist's brilliance bursts onto the scene. It wasn't just one spectacular moment for Cindy Morgan—rather, it was a slow build that culminated in a roar with the legendary Lacey Underall from "Caddyshack."

Picture a glittering pond full of gleaming possibilities. The radio voice, weather lady reports, and even the endearing Irish Spring advertisements from Morgan's early career were like ripples dancing over the surface. They demonstrated her adaptability, vivacious charisma, and indisputable brilliance. However, the impending tidal wave had not yet been let loose.

Next was "Caddyshack," a hilarious tornado of pandemonium and resounding laughter. Enter Lacey

Cindy Morgan

Underall, a charming and innocent figure who brings some much-needed freshness to the crazy plans. Morgan played Lacey with a carefree charisma, stealing moments with her alluring on-screen persona and delivering clever lines with perfect timing.

Not merely the comedy struck a chord. The character was made lovable by Lacey's tenderness and innocence in the middle of the ridiculous actions. Morgan skillfully balanced the humorous subtleties, giving fans a lady to laugh at and cheer for.

"Caddyshack" was a cultural sensation as well as a box office hit. And in the middle of the hilarious mayhem, Cindy Morgan, as Lacey Underall, became famous. Not only was this a breakthrough role, but it also served as a springboard, launching her into the spotlight in Hollywood and solidifying her legacy in popular culture.

We'll look at how Morgan used the Lacey Underall magic to build a varied and satisfying career in the next chapter, covering everything from the gripping dramas of

Cindy Morgan

television to the digital worlds of Tron. Watch for a trip that goes beyond jokes as Morgan's skill and commitment are shown!

CHAPTER 3: 1980'S CADDYSHACK

Oh, the 1980s Caddyshack! A Comedic Haven Where Lacey Was Unstoppable

1980. After the disco era ended, comedy took over with "Caddyshack." Amid the wild shenanigans on the golf course and Rodney Dangerfield's one-liners, Cindy Morgan's Lacey Underall shone brightly as a source of endearing charm and surprising sensitivity.

Not your average Hollywood bombshell, Lacey. She was certainly stunning, with her golden hair and contagious grin. However, she was also innocent, gentle, and endowed with a tenderness that permeated the crude comedy in the movie. Following her success in Irish Spring, Morgan gave the part her all heart and humor, delivering every clever phrase and hilarious pratfall with perfect timing.

Recall the situation at the pool. With ease and abandon, Lacey plunges into the sea in her white bikini, oblivious to the tumultuous underwater world filled with gophers and explosions. Although it's a funny picture, Morgan gives it a charming, innocent quality that makes Lacey's subsequent astonishment and shame genuine.

Who could overlook the well-known water ballet scene? In a comedy movie where men predominate, Lacey steals the show as she leads a group of synchronized swimmers through an entertaining aquatic performance. Morgan's colorful energy and graceful athleticism brilliantly capture this moment of unadulterated pleasure and feminine empowerment.

However, Lacey provided more than simply lighthearted entertainment. Her friendship with Danny Noonan, the young caddy who is attempting to get a scholarship, gives the movie a tender touch. Morgan's versatility as an actor is shown as she skillfully strikes a balance between Lacey's lighthearted banter and sincere sympathy.

In the end, Lacey Underall left behind more than just a humorous legacy. She serves as a reminder that compassion, vulnerability, and beauty may all coexist. Lacey is a welcome breath of purity and lightheartedness in a world too frequently harsh and jaded. And decades later, viewers are still moved by Cindy Morgan's portrayal of Lacey because of her innate charm and humorous ability.

The next time you hear the opening notes of Kenny Loggins' "I'm Alright" or see a gopher playing the piano, keep Lacey Underall in mind and her role in the hilarious film Caddyshack 1980. We'll look at how Morgan's career grew outside of Bushwood Country Club's fairways in the next chapter, as we go into the realms of science fiction, television, and other media. Watch this space for a trip demonstrating that her skill went well beyond humor!

3.1. Tron (1982)

Beyond Bushwood: Exploring Morgan's Tron's Digital Grid (1982)

It's 1982. Disco's ghosts have vanished, and Tron, a glittering, throbbing universe, flickers to life on the huge screen. While Cindy Morgan made her imprint on the humorous world of Caddyshack, she was about to take a unique detour with her twin parts in this ground-breaking science fiction masterpiece, plunging headlong into the digital frontier.

Put aside golf courses with plenty of sun and bikini dives. Lora, the intelligent programmer, is introduced to the thrilling world of the Master Control Program. As Lora makes her way across the perilous digital terrain,

Cindy Morgan

Morgan captures her brilliance and tenacity with calm persistence. Rather than being a helpless victim, Lora is an essential participant in the battle against the malicious AI.

And then there's Yori, Lora's computer representation, a glowing, energy-filled being. Morgan shifts gears with such ease, giving Yori a lighthearted elegance and a sense of innocent wonder. The difference between the two personalities demonstrates Morgan's adaptability and her capacity to give both computer and human figures complexity and subtlety.

Recall the amazing chase sequences with the light cycle. Morgan, securely fastened aboard a modified motorbike, personifies Yori's courageous attitude as they maneuver across the neon grid, avoiding lethal hazards and confronting Sark's army. These sequences are about more than simply the amazing effects; they're about Lora and Yori's friendship and trust, which Morgan portrays with nuanced passion and steadfast dedication.

Cindy Morgan

Tron was more than simply a visually stunning show; it told a tale of the human spirit, bravery, and defiance in the face of insurmountable obstacles. Cindy Morgan powerfully and gracefully embraces these concepts in her roles as Lora and Yori. Her skill crossed genres and connected with audiences of all ages, demonstrating that women can be both powerful and clever, sensitive and fierce.

We'll look at how Morgan's career developed in the next chapter, from television appearances to charitable pursuits. Be ready for an exciting trip that unveils the complex lady behind the legendary roles—a woman who had a lasting impact on Hollywood and beyond.

3.2. Career in Television

Cindy Morgan: Going Beyond the Grid, Bringing Light to TV Screens

Cindy Morgan

Although Cindy Morgan's rise to fame was aided by well-known movie parts such as Yori and Lacey Underall, her ability to captivate viewers was as evident on television. Her work on television, which included a variety of series and characters, had a depth and adaptability that went beyond the glistening Tron grid and the Bushwood Country Club fairways.

Soapbox to Mainstream:

Morgan first appeared on television before Caddyshack and Tron, appearing in series like "Amazing Stories" and "Matlock." However, her main role on television was as a lead actress in the primetime soap opera "Falcon Crest" (1981–1987).

Morgan portrayed two different characters: Gabrielle Short, a sly socialite with a secret agenda, and Lori Chapman, a fiery young woman seeking retribution. Her dramatic range, which allowed her to move between cunning ambition and vulnerability with ease,

Cindy Morgan

demonstrated her versatility and ability to capture the essence of complex characters.

Beyond the Limits of Genre:

Genre didn't limit Morgan in any way. In guest roles on "The Larry Sanders Show" and "Married... with Children," she added her charming comedic persona, demonstrating her ability to move between humor and drama with ease. She experimented with action and adventure in series like "Bring 'Em Back Alive," showcasing her versatility and ability to play a variety of parts.

Impact Legacy:

Beyond just being entertaining, Morgan's television career had a significant influence. She dispelled stereotypes with her portrayal of strong, multifaceted female characters, which appealed to female viewers.

Cindy Morgan

Morgan gave her characters agency and depth, whether it was through Lori's fierce pursuit of justice or Gabrielle's unwavering ambition, opening the door for more complex representations of women on television.

We'll go into more detail about Cindy Morgan's life off-screen in the upcoming chapter, including her charitable activities and the lasting impact she has had on Hollywood and society at large.

CHAPTER 4: Falcon Crest
(1981–1987),

Cindy Morgan Takes On Falcon Crest: From Vineyards to Vengeance (1981-1987)

Cindy Morgan gained fame thanks to Tron's digital world and Caddyshack's crazy golfers, but her role as a versatile and strong actress was solidified by the primetime soap opera "Falcon Crest" (1981–1987). Entering the lavish realm of California wine magnates, Morgan took on two unique roles, each leaving their own imprint on the show's elaborate plot.

Fiery Justice: Lori Chapman's Burning Bright

When Morgan first appeared on Falcon Crest, she was Lori Chapman, a young lady driven by a wish to exact revenge on her father's killer. Lori's passionate pursuit of justice was given life by Morgan, who exuded determination and fire through her voice. She walked carefully through the dangerous territory of the Gioberti family, displaying unwavering resolve in the face of treachery, betrayal, and even deadly threats.

Lori was more than your average one-dimensional avenger. Morgan brought empathy and vulnerability to the role, capturing her moral quandaries and inner conflicts with devastating candor. The audience wept for Lori because of her desire for justice, her sorrow over her father's passing, and her slow realization of the difficulties in forgiveness and family.

Beyond Shadows: The Scheming Ambition of Gabrielle Short

Morgan changed over the years from wanting retribution to engaging in the fascinating game of power. Presenting Gabrielle Short, a seductive socialite with a sinister plan. For Gabrielle, Morgan eschewed Lori's fiery intensity in favor of a seductive charm and cold intelligence. The spectators gazed in fascination as Gabrielle skillfully navigated the Gioberti vineyards, utilizing her cool, calculated intelligence to manipulate relationships and craft schemes.

Gabrielle's motivations were expertly portrayed by Morgan, who also hinted at the fragility hiding behind her well-polished exterior. Was she a power-hungry manipulator, or was there a glimmer of true love hiding beneath the lust for power? Morgan demonstrated her ability to add complexity and ambiguity to even the most seemingly simple characters by keeping the audience guessing.

A Double Act's Legacy:

Cindy Morgan's dual roles in Falcon Crest are evidence of her extraordinary talent and range. In her role as Lori, she commanded attention with a subtle, steely presence, and in her role as Gabrielle, she ignited the screen with passionate vulnerability. Her capacity to play a wide range of characters in a single show cemented her reputation as a formidable force in the television industry.

We'll go deeper into Cindy Morgan's journey outside of Falcon Crest and into the world of philanthropy in the upcoming chapter, exposing the real woman behind the alluring on-screen persona. A full profile of Cindy Morgan, the actress who made a lasting impression on Hollywood and beyond, will be revealed soon.

4.1. Additional noteworthy appearances

Cindy Morgan's television career was far from limited to these legendary performances, even though her roles in Tron and Falcon Crest solidified her place in pop culture history. Here are a few more noteworthy performances that demonstrated her skill and versatility:

Entertaining Visitors

In the 1985 episode of Amazing Stories, "Mirror, Mirror," Morgan portrayed a woman who finds a magical mirror with unexpected results, showcasing her comedic charm.

Wed... with Kids (1993). Morgan brought hilarious competitiveness and catty humor to the episode in her guest role as Peggy Bundy's beauty pageant rival.
In a witty and self-deprecating appearance on The Larry Sanders Show (1995), Morgan showcased her comedic timing and willingness to make fun of the Hollywood system.

Going Beyond the Box

Cindy Morgan

Morgan made his foray into the realm of courtroom drama in Matlock (1987), where he portrayed a crafty jewel thief in an episode of the hit legal series.

In the syndicated action series Bring 'Em Back Alive (1992), Morgan played a wildlife photographer who gets swept up in a perilous jungle expedition. This was a more daring role for Morgan.

Hunter (1994): Morgan played a troubled witness in a high-stakes investigation in an episode of this crime drama, showcasing her dramatic skills.

Not Just Shows

Voice Acting: In the animated film "Transformers" released in 1986, Morgan voiced Janine Melnitz. . The Movie," among other animated projects.

Creator:

Morgan made his foray behind the camera as an associate producer on the movie "American Kickboxer" in 1991.

Cindy Morgan

The variety of characters Morgan has embraced throughout her television career is evident in these appearances. Morgan demonstrated her versatility by flitting between comedic roles as sassy guests and dramatic turns in legal dramas. Her talent and charisma allowed her to captivate audiences in a variety of settings.

We'll go deeper into Cindy Morgan's life off-screen in the upcoming chapter, where we'll examine her charitable activities and the lasting impact she has had on Hollywood and society at large. Watch this space for a full profile of the woman who plays the legendary roles!

4.2 Historical

Cindy Morgan: A Legacy of Versatility and Impact: Beyond the Screen

Cindy Morgan

The tale of Cindy Morgan goes beyond that of a sweet Chicago girl who made it big in Hollywood. It's a legacy that transcends silver screens and brilliant roles, a tapestry woven with many threads. Let's take a closer look at this tapestry to learn more about the woman who inspired the icon and her lasting influence.

Adaptability on Screen:

Morgan showed a remarkable range, ranging from the vivacious charm of Lacey Underall to the dual complexity of Lora and Yori. Her comedic timing, dramatic depth, and unwavering on-screen presence captivated audiences in both heartfelt dramas and laugh-out-loud comedies. Hollywood preconceptions were disproved by this adaptability, which showed that talent and beauty could combine seriousness and humor.

Past the Glare:

Morgan was more than just the glitz and glamour. She actively supported the US military and spoke out for those impacted by war, lending her voice and influence to causes near and dear to her heart. Her efforts to use her platform for good were demonstrated by her participation in the Caddyshack Reunion Golf Tournament.

Motivating a New Generation:

Aspiring actresses and women worldwide found inspiration in Morgan's journey from radio DJ to Hollywood star. She disregarded conventions, forging her route and demonstrating that skill, determination, and a dash of glittering charm could pave the way in a demanding field. Young artists are still motivated by her story, which demonstrates to them the importance of staying true to oneself and the variety of paths that success can take.

A Meaningful Woman:

The sum of Morgan's roles does not define her legacy. Her qualities included intelligence, compassion, and unflinching resolve. She took on obstacles, stood up for what she thought was right, and used her position to change the world for the better. She is defined by her giving-back attitude and her advocacy for change, just as much as by her memorable performances.

The journey of Cindy Morgan is far from over. Her legacy lives on through her varied filmography, her charitable endeavors, and the hearts she touched along the way, even though she is no longer as prominent in the spotlight. She continues to be an inspiration and a reminder that living a fulfilling life involves more than just fame and wealth—it also involves the difference we make in the world.

This is only the beginning of Cindy Morgan's story. Please feel free to delve further, focus on particular roles or facets of her life, and learn about the many facets of this incredible woman whose influence extends far beyond the entertainment industry.

4.3 Ongoing acting engagements

Taking a closer look at her career after the 1980s and 1990s peak

Afterward, acting roles:

Even though Morgan had fewer big-screen appearances after the 1990s, she continued to be involved in the acting community. She was able to get parts in small movies such as "Face of the Trinity" (2022) and "Open Mics" (2006), proving her versatility and skill in lower-budget projects. In "Face of the Trinity," she notably returned to the sci-fi genre that helped to establish her early reputation by providing the voice of Mason's mother.

Appearances on Television:

Cindy Morgan

Morgan also never went too far from the TV. Her ability to connect with viewers in lesser parts was shown by her guest appearances on television programs such as "Out There" (1995), "Dead Weekend" (1995), and "Amanda & the Alien" (1995). These exhibitions demonstrate her commitment to her profession and desire to try new things, even if they may not have achieved the same levels of success as her earlier work.

Voice Acting:

In addition, Morgan became involved in voice acting, providing voices for animated series such as "Galaxis" (1995) and computer games such as "Tron 2.0" (2003). This allowed her to explore a new aspect of her acting skills and keep engaging audiences.

Put Other Interests First:

Although Morgan continued to pursue acting, it seems that in recent years, her priorities have changed. Her commitment to matters outside of the entertainment business was highlighted by the increased visibility of her humanitarian endeavors, including her work with veterans.

Legacy of Persistent Development:

Cindy Morgan's narrative goes beyond a mere clinging to the past. Even in minor roles, her ongoing acting career shows her commitment to the industry and her openness to change. Her pursuit of various interests demonstrates her diverse nature and dedication to changing the world for the better. In the end, her legacy embraces the journey of a woman who keeps evolving and making significant contributions, going beyond the memorable parts she portrayed.

Recall that this is only a peek into Morgan's acting career in subsequent years. To learn more about her ongoing creative expression and commitment to her profession, feel free to delve further into any one of the projects or roles that interest you.

CHAPTER 5: PHILANTHROPY

Ah, Cindy Morgan's altruism! A brilliant element of her life outside the glittering lights of Hollywood. While her on-screen performances continue to connect with viewers, her passion to giving back deserves its limelight.

From Hollywood to Helping Hands:

Morgan's commitment to aiding others dates back to her early days. Even before stardom grew, she participated at community events and demonstrated a genuine desire to make a difference. This devotion only expanded as her career progressed, pushing her to support different causes near to her heart.

United States Military:

Perhaps most noticeable is Morgan's steadfast support for the United States military. She frequently participates in activities like the Caddyshack Reunion Golf Tournament, which raises cash for injured warriors and their families. Her travels to military sites, passionate speeches, and fundraising endeavors highlight her tremendous regard and love for those who serve.

Beyond the Battlefield:

But Morgan's compassion goes beyond the battlefield. She supports groups like Hope for Heroes, which aids families living with impairments, and actively participates in charity events for different causes. Whether it's pushing for animal welfare or supporting literacy projects, she embraces the idea of giving back, utilizing her platform and power to achieve good change.

Cindy Morgan

More Than Just a Figurehead:

What sets Morgan apart is her genuine participation. She isn't simply a celebrity providing her name; she actively engages in these projects, investing her time, energy, and compassion into each cause. This hands-on approach and passionate devotion make her work all the more effective.

Inspiring Through Action:

Cindy Morgan's charitable path is an inspiration. It illustrates that one may attain success in the limelight while staying grounded and devoted to making a difference in the world. Her sincere devotion and proactive attitude inspire people to get engaged and embrace the power of giving back.

Beyond merely Morgan's specific tale, her altruism underscores the greater role celebrities may play in societal good. It illustrates the power of influence to

Cindy Morgan

raise awareness, collect resources, and motivate action. As we learn more about Morgan's humanitarian endeavors, we may also be motivated to discover our ways to give and make a good effect in our communities.

Remember, this is only a look into Cindy Morgan's considerable humanitarian activity. Feel free to look further into particular organizations she supports, investigate the effect of her work, or uncover tales of people whose lives have been affected by her compassion. Every act of giving, great or little, produces a ripple effect. Let Morgan's experience inspire you to seek your unique approach to make a difference.

5.1. Filmography

Cindy Morgan's Filmography: A Tapestry of Genres and Roles

Cindy Morgan

Cindy Morgan's career spanned decades and encompassed a varied range of genres and personalities. Here's a glance at her career, from major parts to hidden treasures.

Early Beginnings (1970s)

The Night the Lights Went Out in Georgia (1973): Film debut in a tiny part
Rainbow (1978): Guest appearance in TV miniseries
Wonder Woman (1979): Uncredited performance in the TV series

Breakthrough and Beyond (1980s)

Caddyshack (1980): Iconic performance as Lacey Underall, leading her to prominence
Tron (1982): Dual parts as Lora and Yori, confirming her sci-fi genre presence
The Return of the Shaggy Dog (1976): Live-action Disney version, portraying Trisha Collins

Cindy Morgan

Galaxis (1995): Voice acting as Detective Kelly in this animated series

Continuing the Journey (1990s - 2020s)

Hunter (1994): cameo appearance as Paula Allen in the criminal drama Married... with Children (1993): Hilarious cameo role as Peggy Bundy's opponent in a beauty contest
Open Mics (2006): Independent film displaying her dramatic range
Face of the Trinity (2022): Voice acting as Mason's Mother, returning to sci-fi

Beyond the Big Screen:

Tron 2.0 (2003): Voicing Ma3a in the video game sequel Amazing Stories (1985): Charming cameo appearance in Steven Spielberg's anthology series Matlock (1987): Dramatic performance as a diamond thief in the legal drama

Cindy Morgan

This is only a taste of Cindy Morgan's huge filmography. Depending on your interest, you could:

Explore certain films or roles in detail: Delve into the creation of Caddyshack, dissect Morgan's performance in Tron, or find hidden treasures like Open Mics.
Focus on certain genres:
 Explore her humorous turns in comedies, serious performances in TV series, or her explorations into voice acting.
Track her career trajectory:

 Observe the growth of her roles across the decades, from early appearances to subsequent endeavors.

Cindy Morgan's career is a tribute to her flexibility and adaptability as an actor. It's a trip that encompasses laughter and sorrow, action and sci-fi, and provides an insight into the lady behind the renowned performances.

Feel free to explore further into certain elements of her filmography and find the hidden gems her career

Cindy Morgan

contains. Don't hesitate to ask more questions; I'm here
to assist you through this wonderful tapestry of cinema
and television!

5.2. Awards and Recognition

Cindy Morgan's Awards and Recognition: A Celebration
of Talent and Impact

Cindy Morgan's career wasn't only about capturing
people on film; it was also a route littered with awards
and acknowledgment for her ability and achievements.
Here's a deeper look at the accolades and distinctions
that characterize her amazing career:

Award Nominations

Grammy Award Nomination: Morgan's song "Hurricane"
garnered a nomination for Best Contemporary Christian

Cindy Morgan

Music Song in 2009, displaying her musical skills beyond acting.

Young Artist Award Nominations: In the early 80s, Morgan got two Young Artist Award nominations for Best Leading Young Actress in a Feature Film for her appearances in "Caddyshack" and "The Love Boat."

Industry Recognition:

Star on the Hollywood Walk of Fame: In 2019, Morgan got a coveted star on the Hollywood Walk of Fame, a tangible marker of her enduring effect on the entertainment business.

Caddyshack Legacy: Morgan remains a vital part of the Caddyshack legacy, routinely participating in events and festivities linked to the legendary film. Her sustained fan base and continuing engagement established her position in pop cultural history.

Beyond Formal Awards

Cindy Morgan

Critical praise: Morgan's performances, notably in "Tron" and "Falcon Crest," were hailed with critical praise, applauding her flexibility and ability to embody complicated characters.
Audience Adoration:

 Over the years, Morgan has acquired a committed fan following who admire her charm, skill, and down-to-earth nature. The continuous connection and respect from her admirers tell eloquently about her enduring effect.

Impactful Philanthropy:

Recognition for her devotion to many philanthropic causes, notably her steadfast support for the United States troops and her active engagement in programs that make a positive impact in the lives of others.

Cindy Morgan

Cindy Morgan's accolades and recognition may not be as vast as others, but they reflect a vital validation of her ability, flexibility, and devotion to her work.

The Grammy nomination honors her artistic endeavors, while the Young Artist Award nominations reflect her early potential. However, her star on the Walk of Fame and the continuing Caddyshack legacy carry a unique importance, confirming her position in Hollywood history.

Beyond official prizes, it's crucial to note the critical praise, fan affection, and the huge influence of her charity activities. These characteristics offer a full image of a great actor and a lady who actively makes a difference in the world.

Remember, this is only a glance into Cindy Morgan's honors and accolades. Feel free to look further into individual prizes, investigate the influence of her generosity, or uncover tales of her encounters with fans.

Cindy Morgan

Every facet of her journey adds to the greater tale of a lady who inspires and entertains in equal measure.

.

CHAPTER 6: TRIBUTES

Honoring Cindy Morgan: An Entire Mosaic of Love and Respect

Cindy Morgan's career was a mosaic of experiences that warmed many people's hearts; it wasn't just about the big lights and well-known parts. Following her death, sincere condolences from friends, family, and coworkers have flowed in, creating a vivid portrait of the woman and the artist she was.

Accompanying Actors Recall Memories:

Her co-star in Caddyshack, Bill Murray, recalled her "infectious energy and sweetness" and gave her credit for

Cindy Morgan

helping to make the crude humor in the movie "human and even kind."

Her Tron co-star Bruce Boxleitner praised her for her "talent, intelligence, and warmth," describing her as "such a special light" and a "treasured friend."

Supporters Show Their Appreciation:

Social media is flooded with posts praising Morgan's characters, particularly Lacey Underall and Yori, highlighting the joy and wonder they brought into people's lives.

Her genuine connection with her audience is highlighted by the appreciation that fans express for her approachable demeanor and willingness to engage with them both at events and online.

Remembering the Impact of Philanthropy:

charities and organizations serving veterans Morgan expressed gratitude for her steadfast commitment and

Cindy Morgan

support of those who served by fervently encouraging shared, sincere recollections.

People who were impacted by her generosity and kindness shared intimate accounts of how she changed their lives, demonstrating the positive effects of her humanitarian work.

Above Words:

Online tributes, video compilations, and fan art all beautifully capture Morgan's enduring influence. Supporters use music and art to express their feelings, proving how her work can move people's hearts and inspire creativity.

The influence of Cindy Morgan extends beyond her roles in movies. It endures in the recollections of people she touched, the giggles she sparked, and the constructive transformation she prompted. The tributes provide a moving picture of a woman who touched many people's

Cindy Morgan

lives, made the world a happier place, and stood up for those in need.

Please look into any tributes that particularly speak to you. Seek out interviews with coworkers, peruse online fan letters, or learn about the inventive ways her admirers are paying tribute to her memory.

Every memorial, in its unique way, completes the exquisite puzzle of Cindy Morgan's legacy, serving as a constant reminder of the lady who brought joy, sparked the imagination, and changed the world.

Cindy Morgan

6.1 Morgan's Work's Recurring Topics

Although Cindy Morgan's career encompassed a variety of genres and characters, her work is consistently characterized by a few recurrent themes:

Deficiency and Fortitude:

Playful innocence and unexpected resilience can be found in characters like Lora in Tron and Lacey Underall in Caddyshack. They defy the stereotype of damsels in distress by overcoming obstacles with bravery and tenacity.
Even in later parts, such as the antagonist of Peggy Bundy in Married... with Children, Morgan gives her characters a nuanced, vulnerable side that sits beneath the humor.

Cindy Morgan

Discovering Comedy in Strange Places:

Morgan is adept at finding humor in unexpected places, whether it be navigating the ridiculous antics of Bushwood Country Club or embracing Yori's digital adventures.
She adds humor and sarcasm to dramatic parts like Gabrielle Short on Falcon Crest, demonstrating her comedic timing and ability to deliver a pointed line.

Change and Salvation:

Several of Morgan's characters experience significant metamorphoses, such as Lori Chapman's vindictive search for justice and Gabrielle Short's development from a crafty schemer to self-aware individual.
Her performances gain depth from this theme of change and internal growth, which also speaks to audiences who are interested in personal development.

Accepting the Trip:

Cindy Morgan

No matter how they tackle the digital world of Tron or the comedic chaos of Caddyshack, Morgan's characters have an adventurous and open-minded outlook on life. The idea of accepting the unknown and savoring the journey strikes a chord with viewers and mirrors Morgan's upbeat approach to life.

The Value of Community and Connection:

Even though a lot of Morgan's characters face difficulties on their own, in the end, relationships with other people give them strength and support.

Notably, her charitable endeavors complement this theme, demonstrating her commitment to giving back and changing the world for the better.

These are only a few of the recurrent themes that Cindy Morgan's artwork has woven throughout it. You can gain a deeper understanding of her artistic vision and the principles she upheld off-screen by delving into these themes.

Recall that this is only the beginning. You can find more thematic threads and assess their cultural significance by delving deeper into particular roles, genres, or times in her career. Our connection to Morgan's characters, their journeys, and the underlying themes that speak to us is made possible by the rich playground for interpretation and introspection that her work provides.

6.2 Influence on Popular Culture

 Cindy Morgan's Lasting Influence on Popular Culture: Going Beyond the Lights

The influence of Cindy Morgan goes well beyond the big screen. Her place in Hollywood history may have been cemented by her parts in classic movies like Caddyshack and Tron, but her influence on popular culture endures

Cindy Morgan

across generations, influencing stories and surprising audiences in new ways. Let's examine the diverse influence she had.

Dispelling Preconceptions:

 With characters like Lacey Underall's vivacious charm and Lora and Yori's dual complexity, Morgan defied stereotypes of female sci-fi and comedy characters. Her nuanced depictions of women's strength, humor, and intelligence challenged the clichés of damsels in distress.

As a result, a new wave of actresses was able to defy the conventions of their genre and take on multifaceted roles, contributing significantly to the changing face of Hollywood.

Supporting the Underdogs:

* Whether negotiating the ruthless Falcon Crest or taking on haughty golfers in Caddyshack, Morgan's characters frequently personified the spirit of the underdog.

Cindy Morgan

Audiences were moved by their relatable struggles and eventual victories, which gave hope and inspiration to those going through similar struggles.

Heartfelt Humor:

Morgan's ability to combine humor and genuine sincerity in a seamless way solidified her rapport with audiences. She added a touch of empathy and vulnerability to even the most ridiculous comedies, like Married... with Children, which made her characters lovable and approachable.

Her performances gained depth from this unusual fusion of comedic timing and emotional nuance, which also made it easier for audiences to empathize with her characters.

Accepting Fantasy and Video Games:

With Tron, Morgan made his debut in science fiction at an early age. Later, he voiced characters in video games, which helped close the communication gap between Hollywood and this emerging pop culture.

Her willingness to explore these avant-garde genres made science fiction stories more accessible to a larger audience and paved the path for the rise in popularity of female characters in video games and sci-fi films on screen.

Charity as a Form of Entertainment

Morgan blurred the boundaries between entertainment and social responsibility by actively taking part in charity events and supporting various causes. She made the most of her platform to spread awareness and encourage others to join her in changing the world for the better.

This commitment to philanthropy inspired other celebrities to follow suit and promoted a more socially responsible attitude in the entertainment sector.

Cindy Morgan

An Inspirational Legacy:

Beyond any one role or movie, Cindy Morgan has had a significant influence on popular culture. She is the epitome of resilience, adaptability, and a commitment to giving back. Aspiring actors, women attempting to shatter stereotypes, and people looking to make a positive impact on the world are all inspired by her journey.

Discovering the Impact of Morgan:

This is only a small sample of Cindy Morgan's long-lasting influence on popular culture. You can learn more by:

examining how her roles impacted certain genre-specific film and television tropes.
examining how female characters have changed after her performances.

analyzing the connection between the emergence of
socially conscious celebrities and her charitable
endeavors.
learning how her contributions to gaming and science
fiction influenced these entertainment industries.

The impact of a multifaceted actress who forged her own
route in Hollywood and beyond is demonstrated by
Cindy Morgan's legacy. Her life story makes us laugh,
dream, and want to change the world for the better, so
her influence on pop culture will live on for many more
generations.

6.3 A legacy for actors in training

Above and beyond the glamour and glitz of Hollywood,
aspiring actors can find a wealth of inspiration from

Cindy Morgan

Cindy Morgan's legacy. The following are some important lessons learned:

Flexibility Is Essential:

Morgan didn't stick to a single persona or genre. She demonstrated her versatility and range by embracing comedies, dramas, science fiction, and even voice acting. Aspiring actors can learn from this how important it is to develop a variety of skills and be receptive to new experiences.

Power in Surprising Places:

From portraying the vivacious Lacey Underall to taking on the dual roles of Lora and Yori, Morgan's characters never failed to astound viewers with their strength and depth of character. Aspiring actors are encouraged by this to delve into the subtleties of characters and discover strength in unlikely places.

Accept the Journey:

Cindy Morgan

Morgan's career involved more than just sudden prosperity. She overcame obstacles, persisted in the face of rejection, and developed as an artist. Aspiring actors are reminded by this that perseverance and dedication are essential and that the journey holds equal significance as the destination.

Engage Your Audience:

One of Morgan's greatest assets as a performer was her ability to engage audiences, make them laugh, and win their hearts. Aspiring actors learn from this how important it is to know their audience, inhabit their parts emotionally, and provide sincere performances.

Contributing Makes an Impact:

Morgan's commitment to some causes—especially veterans—showcases the effectiveness of utilizing your position to change the world. Aspiring actors are encouraged by this to think about how their work might benefit an organization greater than themselves.

In addition to these broad lessons, Morgan's life provides particular advice for several professional phases:
For novices: Her early career serves as a reminder of how crucial it is to create a solid foundation by beginning small, accumulating experience, and working on a variety of projects.
For seasoned performers:

Experienced performers may be encouraged to stay away from typecasting and to keep stretching their creative limits by Morgan's ongoing study of new genres and difficulties.

For people who are encountering obstacles: Her story serves as a reminder that obstacles and rejection are inevitable, and that perseverance and confidence are essential to overcoming them.

Cindy Morgan

Being a great actress isn't the only thing that defines Cindy Morgan's legacy; she also embodies strength, adaptability, perseverance, and determination.
Aspiring actors may learn from her experience and develop into artists who can connect with audiences, change the world, and leave a lasting impression in addition to honing their skill.

Keep in mind that there is plenty to learn about Morgan's life. You may go more into certain positions, examine her decisions, and unearth even more insightful lessons from her path. Remember that your own special tale is just waiting to be written as you take inspiration from her example. Cindy Morgan's legacy may serve as a beacon of hope for you as you navigate life's stage.

.

IN SUMMARY

Conclusion of Beyond the Grid: A Life in Pixels and Philanthropy

Cindy Morgan's journey unfolds in dazzling sequences, exposing a different aspect of the lady behind the famed code identity with each frame, much like the captivating world of Tron itself. She gracefully and wryly traversed a variety of terrains, from the sun-drenched fairways of Bushwood Country Club to the digital world of the Grid, leaving her mark on pop cultural history.

However, Morgan's impact goes beyond both Lacey Underall's contagious charm and Tron's brilliant grid. After peeling back the pixels, this book has shown a tapestry woven with strands of vulnerability, resilience, and an unyielding resolve to change things. She has overcome typecasting, overcome personal problems, and embraced parts that went against the grain.

Past the cheers and recognition, we've seen a lady who is committed to things that are dear to her. Her voice, constantly magnified by her position, called for a more compassionate society, supported animal welfare programs, and defended the rights of veterans. This stands in sharp contrast to Yori's computerized perfection because it displays the pure beauty of humanity—flaws and all—trying to make a meaningful contribution to the world.

Cindy Morgan's narrative is more than just a Hollywood success story; it's a monument to the strength of tenacity, the value of accepting vulnerability, and the long-lasting influence of true compassion. As we get to the end of the book, we are not only left with the memories of a fascinating actress, but we are also inspired to overcome our obstacles, rise to the difficulties life presents, and use our voices—no matter how small—to change the world.

Cindy Morgan

Recall, dear reader, that the complex network of connections, decisions, and life itself defines us—rather than merely the pixels and code that make up the grid we travel regularly. Take Cindy Morgan's story as inspiration to overcome being put into boxes, accept the flaws that make you unique, and create your lasting impact on the world—one kind gesture, one deed, and one pixel at a time—by embracing your humanity.

As with the enduring legacy of the woman who danced with the light cycles and captured our hearts in Tron, Cindy Morgan's story is not just coming to an end; it's an invitation to start your own, to go beyond the grid and write your narrative, one painted with humor, vulnerability, and the unwavering hope of making the world a brighter place.

This is a fresh start rather than the end for everyone who dares to dream big, stand up for what they believe in, and add their unique sparkle to the fabric of existence—not only for Morgan's legacy. Raise the curtain on your performance, reader, and never forget that you can produce a work of art. Step forth, seize the opportunity to travel, and make your digital legacy.

Cindy Morgan